DRAG

Duriel E. Harris

ELIXIR PRESS

DRAG

Acknowledgments

The author gratefully acknowledges the editors of the following publications in which some of the poems in this collection originally appeared or are forthcoming: *580 Split*: "Q (on five)" and "Phaneric Display No. 3: Slumber Party Cabaret"; *African American Review*: "Brown Sugar," "Crazy Woman Blues," "Drive," "Recess," "seeing the dead: lucky seven," and "Voice of America"; *fyah.com*: "seeing the dead: seventh night," "seeing the dead: who call on occasion in dream," and "Twin-Mother, Woman Tree"; *nocturnes (re)view of the literary arts*: "drag," "drone," "feed," "Monday," and "Phaneric Display No. 2: The Meta"; *Voices Rising*: "Gravity"; *Cave Canem IV*: "Villanelle for the dead white fathers"; *Cave Canem VI*: "and the women with angry hair sit clapping or Nationalism."

"what we have lost" first appeared in *Spirit and Flame: An Anthology of Contemporary African American Poetry* (Syracuse University Press). "Awakening: Proem and Creation" first appeared in *Step Into a World: A Global Anthology of the New Black Literature* (John Wiley & Sons). "Water from the Well" first appeared in the *Bum Rush the Page* (Three Rivers Press). "A Secret, Fatal Line" first appeared in the *Urban Life Center 2003 First Voices Calendar*. "Drive" also appears in *Role Call: A Generational Anthology of Social and Political Black Literature & Art* (Third World Press).

Special thanks to the following organizations whose generous grants have made my work possible: The Illinois Arts Council, Cave Canem Foundation, Chicago Bar Association.

In gratitude to all that is, I wish to extend blessings to my parents, family and extended family, fellow artists, poets and friends, with particular notes of appreciation to Sterling D. Plumpp, Michael Anania, James C. Hall, Barbara Ransby, James Park Sloan, Jennifer Devere Brody, and Michael Lieb for their fundamental guidance and to Black Took Collective, Yolanda Wisher, and Abe Louise Young for their insight and editorial assistance.

Elixir Press is a non-profit literary organization.

ISBN: 1-932418-00-8

Cover Photo: *(W)rap*, Dawn M. Joseph, Polaroid transfers
Cover Design: Collin Hummel
Author Photo: Stephen Garrett

Elixir Press
P. O. Box 18010 • Minneapolis, MN 55418
www.elixirpress.com • *info@elixirpress.com*

Contents

4th movement

5th movement

sister of famous artist brother
stabbed to death
imagine the pain.

sister of famous artist brother
rolled out on a stretcher
oh what a shame.

sister of famous artist brother
in a black body bag
oh what a drag.

                    —Cheryl Clarke

```
/-`|/-|/-|/-
/--
`/-|`/

/-`|/-|/-|/-
/`--|/-
/||--/

/-`|/-|/-|/-
--/||`-/
/||--/
```

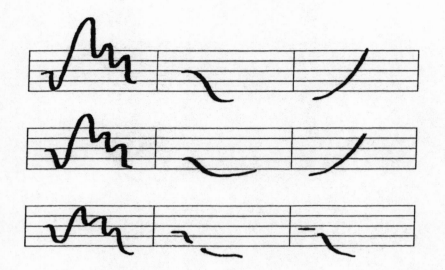

Drag

Opus 4

1st movement

Sonho meu   sonho meu/ Vai buscar quem mora longe sonho meu
—"Sonho Meu" (as performed by Maria Bethania and Gal Costa)

To be frank, I am holding her destiny in my hands and yet I am powerless to invent with any freedom: I follow a secret, fatal line. I am forced to seek a truth that transcends me.... But who can tell if she was not in need of dying?
—Rodrigo S.M., writer and narrator speaks of his principal character Macabea Clarice Lispector's *The Hour of the Star*

A Secret, Fatal Line
(Ten Hundred Block of Racine Avenue, Chicago, IL)

want. unfurls from the spine.

trashy squat. folding
nylon lawn chairs. goodwill
card table, griddle plate,
sugar packets, ashtray. warped
plywood floor. soiled mattress
beneath a sill. something
turning sleep against the wall.

*the hand that feeds
smites and is done.*

the woman who stayed here:
hairless. not a single stringy strand. (except
stray eyelashes) she drew on
half-bird eyebrows to go out, and to church
of god militant pillar and ground of truth
she wore a ratty marcel wig. mahogany.
her soft stink waits on doorknobs and edges.

knew what she wanted. all the w's
sewn into her lining. soldier and willing.
eyes fixed on some point
beyond. no one will go
looking for her gnarled ash.
no one will go looking for a street
hype, homeless black hooker,
who worked her hustle like a wall
street broker. going broke for bulk.
rock smoke. gone in 15 min.

composition by field.
the crease her body made disappearing.

Q
(on five)

rupture : slow leak

this happened, happens, will

grin

>   walk home in straight lines
>   stopwatch yourself

very impressive

fuck to keep the water in
or drink more water

Living Body

: kettle engulfed in heat.
A most casual boil dubs eerie sound, tracks
my horror (buxom, pink) with soap scum.
A slippery bar leaps at the drain:
the monstrous slasher's cue
to yank the curtain to steam.
Flick, shadow, switch. My brown skin
scrubs into gray sudless streams, shower
blasted itch. The body, a scoured pot's gleam:
atingle, aprickle, raw. Vicious
pulse scraping surface and quick
as histamine to needle bites, I lose
twelve years

        to loofa threads and boyscent
cockspunk clinging follicles, laddering
to nest, oily miners erupted into city
through asphalt, legs teasing sewer.

What the mind gives back: pus-bellied,
weighted with stones, crawling
with damage, come to bank
because it must.

        I don't want this
body,
    the body wants me.

ii.
porous.
porthole.
portrait.

iii.
the way the third I stands apart
I
            was received by the body

iv.
water redeems
            erodes
                        contains

v.
living
body
takes
a little
at a time
you almost
don't
notice
soil pulling at soil

vi.
What I learn
I keep.
Face.
Imprint.

drag\…\row of hooks *under* crisp black umbrellas *napping* my head mowing dreams' terse air *arrives* at
BATS(') psychedelic coatroom nigga lips thinned for flight and hanging *breathable fabric* pawpad
BATfaces *unshut* leech like humming sacred *eeeek* rise cube my head: juice-out, they disperse, eating my
locs, body sleighing back dense *flagflap flagflap* (laggard brake slugging) *flagflap flagflap* (tether,flesh

drone \ *rrrrrrnnnnn*\ [dream matter, action—more at HOARD] **a:** weld mask scrip (lust: blunt force ragged *maw* lock and subtle grind *wears away at* clawcuffs pin wrists *wrest* centerbones: fixed: X, petal lids **b:** strident descant *growl* mantra-bloom of my present: succubic coup de theatre: beauty *trapped* bell jar of skin beneath *moaning* NOW IS THE WINTER THE WINTER *warning* violet and sharp **c:** shape viscous tempest press without pith weights *legion* upon me rides permission *rrrrmmmm may we?*— *WIS, you shall receive*

feed \ this, my body (unknown) \[*Am* rite: honoring braid, twisted hemp, and catgut whip] : severed hands tossed to dogs they would pray *o   luminous salvage   o tender*   worshipping fragrant block *oil* warn wood   *o gallop starch and bluing* prod and shepherd scourge they would race chase the dangle singing   *Joy!* and *Onward!* torch cross char *o blessed* part bone from flesh redeem chaff from wheat *fresh heart* to the Governor calling   *Bid! Full hind!* round rump shank—*lips they clipped for keeps*

Monday

she eats an hour and a half dreaming fish
feathered halibut blackened du jour
dogpaddling mustard lake
trailing mangy down
headless and beyond reach

it's three o'clock, glue eyes
younger bro barrels   slumming home after school
dive tuck and roll into blanket-dark
where she sleeps smoking free Salems
trying to catch fire

vial parade and customary fanfare
today was Medical Card Day
is still   a piece left to its slimy tail
hedging minutes' minus
in slow mo

in one dream there's no microwave

in another   next door shampoo girl straddles barstool counter breakfast
like a headline   her hands and soap clouds sun ray
from a blue lead gown   a brickish bow stains her shoulder
so tiny
where the words run together

: overeighteen nomeds notimeouts aidofficeorbust

straight shot on the CTA hinge
windows flapping
Big Green's wings

three fifteen
she scans the street
spots her mother juggling numbers
investing the day's hustle gravy
from barbershop bid at Lee's Chicken and Liquor
she is hungry

the ceiling fan whirs but doesn't turn
Bigcat claws a thought-
missing slipper into gutted rat and Peanut
Tia Maria's bighead baby Momma sits on weekdays
has escaped the playpen again
is gushing himself into a linoleum square
mimicking his abuelita's watery dementia
ay mi'ja no puedo mas
back and forth across mud patch grass

fickle trickle
he pee paints baseboard cracks
like an Orkin cherub earning snatch
by the pull-ups

pigeon shit

It's a set up.
                    —the infamous Tasha Thomas,
                      Chicago drag performer,
                      M(istress) of Ceremonies,
                      and honorary lesbian

Figures

Phaneric Display No. 1:
Patricia "Han'le It" Johnson
Checkerboard Lounge, Chicago, IL

Looky hyeah looky hyeah
mister notepad mister slick
bleachbone buckra critic n shit:
got a whetstone and a straight razor
flat silver spine and loose jive
bumping bulbs of smoke
'gainst a congenital itch.

Picked yo number
from the wilderworld craw
rubbing snake bellies wit possum fat
wouldya believe that mister professor
though crow rags knottin my brow
with shine: totin dis pan, drivin dat mule
like a black baptist woman on the Sabbath.
You ain't got but one face, gazer;
I know you: our people go long ways back.
It ain't water what runs 'tween us.
Spirit songs, ragtime, and jazz
jazz and the white critic
jazz and crack-o-ass funk
jook grind shimmy blade. Shit,
cut the cake cut the rug and yo neck
and dare the law to slip 'round mine.

Looky, hyeah's yo learnin:
no matter how low down yo dance,
we ain't that tight, call me out
my name and I'll pull yo card so fast
you'll spin like a fool with a wooden nickel;

I'll put you down like a shot.
I will.

Phaneric Display No. 2:
The Meta

The intellect must be taught | extremities are first to go babythataway™ | red scotch plaid skirts and vests kneesocks and peterpan collars | poppa wheelie into dream poppa rave cap and cruise | blank as normal templates' throaty viral erasure | intellect is the primal faculty | plucked swollen like a muscle | guitar neck cave secret hand-thrown into a shallow bowl | blood cooling to jelly on the blue rim | where you have been collecting | *you need not know the name of a thing to know it* | pinkseamed joint and toes the child will chop the blonde | mop to sheer plugs and plastic until the frames collide | but she's always looked like that

and raggedy ann™ and raggedy andy™

Phaneric Display No. 3:
Slumber Party Cabaret
in E minor

Dear Martha,
I got problems. For one, Andre, maa baby daddy,
is stayin gone half da night. For two, when he do
come home, he cryin broke, claimin he ain't got
no loot to put in on my ALIZE. To top it off
he cain't get wood. So now I'm tense, horn-nay,
and I cain't sleep a wink. If dat don't beat all,
whas really wizack is dat alluvasudden
maa BESTEST friend Shayna "da Hater" is woh out
N lit up every mornin when we git together
to watch YOUNG & the RESTLESS (on her
bootleg TV). She B lookin all wile N smellin
like da bar AND da afta party. I got a stanky-ass
suspicion dat her N Andre is doin da nasty
on maa clock and dat he buyin her broke ass
licker wit maa diaper money. I wanna tear out dat
bitch weave and beat her ass wit da tracks
but I'm on parole and I ain't goin back inside
for da likes of dat saggy tit ho.

> ALL FUCKED UP,
> Laquisha

Dear Laquisha,
Well, you know what they say: "no money
no wine, no lovin' in time". But "tearing hair"
is not the answer. Try couples counseling,
pro bono: watch *Dr. Joy Brown* and Tuesdays'
Oprah. If all else fails consult your local video
store and rent *Delores Claiborne*.

Rest easy, my dear. There are ways.

> All the best,
> Martha S.

Kiss my ass, on the pank.
> —Flame Monroe,
> Chicago drag performer, M(istress) of Ceremonies,
> Comedienne, & Radio Personality

Phaneric Display No. 4:
Feelin Moody˜

Lemme Tellya, Lemme Tellya, Lemme Tellya

SAVE   IT.

I'M NOT   FEELING

U.

TODAY.

---

^[vocal score]

*   I was feelin very mellow   walkin down the street
**   Happiness is in the pursuin   Don't you get bored with what you're doin
*** You laugh at me   and you got the nerve   to criticize   yeah

*   you see I was goin to see my baby   and he makes me feel real moody, like this...[1]
**   Every bite ain't worth the chewin   And the pleasure principle is for wooin[2]
*** If I were you   I'd sit down   and consider what you're doin[3]

~geometric equivalent: "In a Sentimental Mood" as performed by
  Duke Ellington and John Coltrane
[1] from "Feelin Moody" as performed by ESG
[2] from "Pleasure Principle" as performed by Parlet
[3] from "Born This Way" as performed by Carl Bean

2nd movement

Brown Sugar

I dream about you:
raw sugar eyes, skin,
hair, fading in waves
of spoiled water.
Black bubbles rise
from your lips,
sit hardening,
boils on the ocean's skim.
Your body fights
itself, pulling
at the seams,
splitting, gorged to spasm,
breaking to spume and spray.
You can't swim.

I am afraid for you
even though you assure me
you can take the world's shit
and spit it out.
Sixteen, Latin, Black,
queer manchild,
I want to warn you:
you are not the first.
History parts asscheeks
like a mythic sea,
it'll catch you
off guard, boy; take a limb,
a lung, your memory, your sleep.
Your memory.
Your sleep.

Song to the Lover

I.
How long will it take
for the knot of bruised blood
on my left temple to be completely
reabsorbed, how long for the vise
of your skull to loosen
and the dull ache to fade.
Bare knuckle bone against face
flesh. Tender fist kisses.
These are the gifts we exchange
that bind us one to the other,
to secrecy.

II.
Somewhere a match is struck
then put out. A bruise begins
red and swollen on the skin
then the deep purple cools
to dull smokey black. Slowly
reabsorbed into the blood
stream, taken back into torso,
face. Our dance of blows
is similarly governed: a primal
tongue. Together we must decode
each strike to the head; each
cheek and eye, nose and lips,
thin-skinned temples;
determine the grammar of strangulation.
Is it odd that our breasts escape
notice?

III.
Lover: made from pulp of Father and Mother,
semen, ovum, saliva of the first wet kiss.
Lover: made from wild current of family
rising smoke, the fecal stench of rage,
once small and growing yet more powerless;
made from the bend of the tree-limb switch,
solder of extension cord, thick fiberglass
paddle, fine-grain brown leather belt
squared with heavy brass buckle, and finally
the meaty hands of palms and fingers.
Lover: made from world and memory of world.

IV.
O the power of the word-fist.
We need not speak this way.
The body gives first knowledge of war
in the cell. We are
more than the body.
We are poets.
We sing also of the soul.

Powder

I am re-singing this from the underspace
I've been going into for so long.

I could blame it on the music, pounding
in clubs and back alleys where the tantrum
of my drinking fevered into glitter, capillaries
yielding in their tiny throbbing,
or my mother, how she was made,
and her desperate attachment to things,
the way I was like an idea, something
she thought up while reading, that they discussed,
for which my father consented to pay;
the way they strolled through me
on their way: the father,
who had long before and decidedly seen
enough, the mother afraid to look
with no stomach for it.

*   *   *

Oh. She is so
laid back
she could be nodding
but her hands
slender as her body:
she is sleek.
Poised at the lip
of the bar, people
bring her drinks and gossip;
her laugh, manicured
sliver, cautions the tip
of her throat. Tonight
we see each other, nod
slight smiles.
It is enough for me:
I keep dancing.

I am full. Tequila, a beer chaser, dance in place,
another beer, the buzz kicking in nice.

Dominique, my girl, is away
with Butter, her ace. Somewhere out west,
tempting short skirts with their swaggers,
being fine and Louisiana and butch,
pulling lip whiskers they do not have,
two baby gangsters waging bets,
signaling each other. Low budget:
Dominique and me, Butter and Donna—
her girl, my friend by default—doing it
in one room. I am shy. Dominique insistent.
Butter has already started. Donna seems used to it.

They are close
to thirty and we are not yet
twenty: the missing
ten years a gulf wide enough
for anyone to fall through.
They make money to buy cars,
go out, style, keep young girls—
like us—interested. We are usually
four together. Doubled.
Dominique and Butter, huddled,
scheming. Donna and I bored.
They have left us—unwatched—so we are
excited, come to the club every night this week.

Tonight we drive separate cars
in case one of us wants to:
they'll be back tomorrow night.
Donna has Butter's steel blue two seater.
I have mother's new black shiny thing:
leather interior, power everything automatic,
sun roof, bass speakers, perfect for lake driving,
expressway curves. Idle now in an attended lot.

I should roll in it while its still early. Let her have me by the pier.

Jack the speaker, half-spin on the banister, another beer to keep cool, bottle sweat
across my forehead, in the v of my neckline.
Glance over to the bar but the woman is gone.

I don't miss Dominique.

The guy behind me grinds a shine on my ass
and there's no room anywhere. I go
find Donna working the back bar, chatting up Elaine:
skinny, always high. Now to the bathroom steamy with booster queens
playing diva, masking stubble, tucking, and prancing eyelashes:
casual greetings. We squeeze past to the last stall:
the only one with a door. It's big enough for all three of us—
we're small girls, except Donna has a big ass and Elaine has big tits.
I have neither. Donna giggles: she scored enough for the whole night.
Bag. Razor blade. License. Steady hands.
Elaine organizes lines on the toilet top. Donna calls me baby,
feeds me first. I don't pull right, milk dust dribbles my lip.
I pull it all the second time. Left side. Dab.
Donna is much quicker.

The music is loud.

I am high and full and I feel cocky, bitchy and mean and I dance like that,
like I want to fight—elbows jabbing, eyes cutting.
C'mon muthafuckas, I want to scream
but no one wants any of it.

What else?

The woman has sent Elaine for me. I follow.
Upstairs. A knobless door I have never seen,
locked. Code knock—oh—passageways
of rough mortar and cinder block, sawdust floors.
Cliques of weed heads flicking lighters at spliff ends.
Down the hall, around the corner: low light,
a table, chairs. I am delivered and abandoned.
Kiss, Kiss. Cheeks and lips. Mmm, closer. High already above nice.
Two conical excellently rolled joints. No seeds.
Pungent sweet incense. Cigarettes laced with powder. Cold beer, bottle sweat.
Downstairs together. I dance. She courts the bar.
2 or 3 a.m. Not enough party left. Bathroom, stall with door,
kissing and hands across, on—oh—in everything.

What else?   I am only less bored.
Don't waste it—my voice breezes. I hang in the sky
looking down at top of my head, pointed and soft as if I am just born.
Things look right, crisp: framed film stills, sliced sharp.
I am awake now.

She wants me to come home with her for the better than nothing.
Besides I'm shitty, cannot drive. It's true: I am a shake away from sick,
my eyelids droop with revelation. —Oh— We are seeing each other
clearly: She has a plan for everything.
I've already been had.
But I want her to take it from me.

I should drive home and park my mother's car
black and shiny and still tingling from sunrise
in front of her house. I should be thinking about Dominique,
let it all fall back into place with daylight.

Music pumping an interlude of drink, smoke and powder.
Cut to the lake,
her kitchen table,
counter top,
shower,
living room floor,
bed,
window for everyone to see.   I want it:

piled upon itself
so high, a tenement
crowding the sky
and the rumbling of my sadness
as deep beneath, aspiring
towards a magnificent bottom.

Five Days

They come in many shapes but always blah. Wash-worn
white coats, sponges of all-day saliva, nesting
corners of gauze tape smiles. They are preened and pimped

learning to be doctors, and near ninety, you are two weeks
dying, so they wake you to ask your symptoms, how you are
feeling this day, if you want something. You favor

the edge of the bed, calling it the last frontier,
death's thick lip, pursing a double-faced mouth.
Could they lower the rails? Pedal the mattress out of the sink

hole. Ice chips left to water. They give you five days
if the chemo doesn't take. Your wayward uterus
has hitched back home in sheaves, husked

mass-seeds sprayed into fallow. *Fortune rests
in Providence after a few good years*, you tell them,
I'm not afraid to die. This round thinks

you are brave. They have not yet heard
the land churning its coarse fruit.

Gravity

He said he had cancer. He did.
But it was what he did not have that killed him.
It's like that. *Gravity takes.*

The flesh of his body thinned.
Skin fell in flakes.

Nothing left to fight...
We stood on the platform's yellow line,
waiting, rocking our heels, watching
the dingy glint of tracks for signs.
I saw a rat darting in and out of side pockets
pulling twine to make something underground.
I'm unraveling, he said.
I wished I had hopped the turnstile:
as if stealing small things
could bring small things back.

For to him that is joined to all the living there is hope.... For the living know that they shall die: but the dead know not anything

—Ecclesiastes

seeing the dead

seeing the dead
seventh night

Busy against wakefulness
she quilts mysticism for comfort:
fantastic, spade black snatches
cinnamon fringed, dusted gold
shimmers and slow incense.

For six nights candles burn.
Sequined in bells and steady dim,
her hands—almost birds—throw off
their feathers
                              and they come
as if from under water or heavy cloth,
appearing in the quiet half-madness
of death. Strange and familiar
haints, flesh-caped and self-conscious,
emerging from veiny blue milk and mist.

I wonder what they bring her.

seeing the dead
who call on occasion in dream

Stringless marionette
folded in the seam between
upright and prone, glistening
like Kahlo's paper skeletons.
I try to place him outside of fear
but his body forms a question
I cannot answer: I know this,
even in dream.

He wears a jacket and tie,
vest and handsewn Italian loafers—
everything camel: the color of his face.
Even his hair, grown out in baby fine
wisps. But that soft about him
kissed by purple: creeping ivy twists
along his neck,
                              and on my stomach and thighs
the flaky whiteness between my toes
on the lips of my anus, tickling my scrotum
and in the tear ducts.

I turn away.

If I had been a liar
my children would be knitting their hair.
I would have been a good father
but still a sissy.
Don't trip on this latest tragedy.

His voice focuses out an octave
fades to grainy to splash to empty crack.

When I reach for him, I am laced and lovely—
goddess licking ashtrays in a big fine house.

seeing the dead
en route to Town Hall
New York, New York

Dry leafy October,
thin night, full of pockets.
Keys, a stray mint, tobacco
grinds, a sometimey lighter
and tokens. I am one
of the walkers, puffing
crosstown alongside a bus.

Damp and bookish faces pass
in the whirring. This business.
Jacket, tie, indifferent sip.

When I arrive I will cough,
urinate, brush past the sink,
pick lint and dust the hall with hellos.
Skeletons will frenzy about the podium.

But now I am one of the walkers,
smooth mango pit, slipped
from a quick mouth, backpedaling
to brake into intersection.

seeing the dead
lucky seven

Field-wading like a swoll' gut heifer,
she's a mule husk in a sack dress
dragging a plough: old hair and cussy eyes.
With that skinned burlap strap
slung over her shoulder
and a trail behind, sprouting
knotty tubers and loose teeth.

Once she was a woman dreaming, boiling
rice in a borrowed pot. Starched
slip and hosiery. Leaning out of
numbers-wadded windows.
Narrow city, narrow street, sad and narrow
row house—shoddy deck of narrow rooms.
A woman getting by, gnawing at the marrow
of someone else's extra.

Dust turns aside in her mouth,
field-wading down to the last:
rolling eyes for seven,
hemming spring sod and scraps,
blind to left-heaven's bustle
of frost and craps.

seeing the dead
a masque

There is no poetry in courting
justice. Only waiting
and its particular tedium:
hammer marrying skull
in equal measure, drudging
procession of tragicomic masks.
And from above a requiem:
This is how it has always been.

So say the dead, clamorous at my ears.
They ferry across my knotty locs
as I sleep, scattering riddles
from a burnished clay pot, until dreams'
smooth surfaces are grainy and ashen gray.

So it is with us and the camera's eye:
concert of senators and statesmen,
our glory songs screeching law
liberty justice. Sallow rag
of presidency, wrung dry
and brittle. We are a people
bored with living, marking time
in sound bytes, donning hollow
gorgon heads to accuse and rush
enemy stones. Fields of rock.
Sparks and limb-shards where we rub
against each other, touching.

Twin-Mother, Woman Tree

for M.D.

Four-story trees more than a hundred years round
grow toward the street middle where brownstones sit
buddha-open to light like lotus flowers, reaching
toward the sun's white candle, plunging into earth
and sewers and the subway's steel and concrete tunnel.

The A local's sweaty crawl carries me home to Brooklyn.
I ride in the head car, near its eyes, to be visible.
What man can protect a woman he cannot see?
Today it's too hot to trust the train's belly faces:
summer's mean stroke has hacked away at sense.
We cannot eat in it, sleep in it, think in it.
Riot heat, swollen with appetite and fickle.
Best to be vigilant, keep to myself.

First horse out of the gate, I'm slapped by station musk:
dank-cooled funk with a shot of ammonia backwash.
I hold my breath, avoid the handrail, take piss-waxed steps
two at a time up into vibrant air: quarter loosies,
muddy-haired mango pits, bodega merengue jerking feet and hips
and slipping off the Auto Shop's oily corner tires, doorway
hoodies, timmed and unbuckled, softening forty bags in their grips,
crack vial sprinkles, screetch and hustle-murmur *fast money*
hoopty-plush, livery cabs' strawberry candy dashboards
careening dancehall down to Flatbush fruit carts, open air
discounts, bootleg videos, Yankee caps, blank tapes and Hip Hop.
Everything is drunk.
           There's no straight line to my house.
Brooklyn is a friendly hand of detours. Miles long carnival
in the kitty and as many partners as a body can take.

I remember the heat and decide to go home, turn my back
to Fulton Street's restless tossing and walk on South Oxford
just to pass Niki's house.
                              She is self-willed
from the ground, like the trees she calls by their names
who answer in ritual. Root woman, green-winged
cockatoo, she sings me out of my frenzied despair. I buzz
number six but Niki is away: on the train, in Prospect Park,
on Bergen Street, in Philly, uptown, somewhere else,

but I am a mess of hunger, sweat and rising confusion so I sit,
idle, on her stoop. I want to be still, to go upstairs
where I am drawn to myself, where I take in what is good,
what I have little taste for except it's shaped by Niki's hands:
broiled tofu, rice, brown as Brooklyn's summer skin, husked
like footsoles come August, libations, Nina Simone's deep sugar
and Cassandra Wilson's soothing, liquor-sloppy collards,
yoga's expansive breath, yellow grits, and textures of peace.

Niki is a painter, a dancer, earth daughter. For her
everything is spirit: remnant, scrap, found bone,
blood memory, stone. Everything, spirit.
I run my mind along borders of what she has made:
portraits in rickety wooden window frames, collage
splintering mantle, buddha-heart and red splash
aura near James Baldwin's eyes, still damp
on the wall. I remember   *nous nous caryons: we believe*
of ourselves, in ourselves, labret jewel, tribal markings
and chord of Cherokee chant etch flesh
where ancestors catch hold
and shake her:
                    wise protectors they are sending
                                        serenity it resounds.
Her body, visible imprint of prayers' desire.
Woman attuned to beauty and ancestral wisdom,
inheritance I cannot hear over my own insistent noise. So I sit
on the stoop beneath trees and summer's thick blanket
of light, staring into the sun: a green-winged cockatoo
plucking its feathers, calling its twin-mother home.

3rd movement

what we have lost

can you hear it

faint echo/ vespers from the book of ancestry/ once bound & sealed/ melismata/ catalyst for the slow backward wind

fashioned/ blood tooth & bone from earth/ we now stand erect/ evolved from the cell vestiges of what was/ before residue like oil on fingers/ a lingering sourness/ familiar & elusive

something is falling/ I try to remember/ ... / I was a little girl once/ my body a smooth board of flesh

in family photographs/ wearing mother's hats/ she was always smiling/ for the camera/ loved taking pictures/ loved men & daddy's winter wing tips/ loved men/ smiled & teased at their bristly faces/ poked at their soft undersides/ loved men & their long-muscled laps

it was there she played/ her favorite game with daddy/ trapped in the nooks of his arms/ "gotcha" he would say/ "you'll never get away"/ one quick wiggle/ a squirm/ & poof!/ she would escape

delight roasting in almond eyes to see daddy/ grin/ searching the space where she had been/ one blind hand stirring the pot/ *where did she go?*

I was a little girl once/ I see in her family photographs/ smiling & laughing with the men & lanky boys/ unguarded/ her arms swing/ she fills the frame

I pass my hands over my breasts/ hair damp between my legs/ my sex/ soft sponge of buttocks/ It is dark because my eyes are closed/ I am small/ the air a swathe of cotton/ I am still/ I feel them moving their bodies through me/ into mattress/ floor/ wall behind me/ lips brushed with sweat salt/ I taste them in my ears/ the air thick with their pounding/ the sea the river/ my skin/ wet & slick/ feverish/ separates into molecules/ all of the blood to the surface/ to the surface

there were years in between

I was a little girl once/ I want to speak this into being/ soft skull & gristle/ fallen into the world/ before I could know to fear/ to flee/ before I could recognize the act/ name it and its owners/ push them out of me/ through the mirror/ now we are one flesh that knows no boundaries

memory-traces/ white wisps of chalk dust on a child's wiped slate/ standing again before the glass/ who can be certain/ what we have lost/ is worth calling back

and the women with angry hair sit clapping
or Nationalism?

I'd like to dedicate this piece I been workin
to all the sistas in the house.

"The Corner: Johnson

"He don't sell NOTHIN

"no purple felt prayer cloths
mardi gras beads
no second-hand shoes, furniture, women
no tracts in red and black
or fat gilded leaf books with green leatherette covers
not even incense

"mornings he carries a rusting frame folding chair
the gashed vinyl seat reveals provocative vanilla
foam stuffing that leads him through the torn back seat of
his father's old Buick to the damp triangle
joining a black girl's thighs: heaven
he sets up shop to the east and recites
his favorite poems until dusk

"some passersby think he's slow-lucked
drop sweaty coins between his legs
into the seat cushion
reg'lars bring him lunch from Pearline's

"today
a burly shiny-purple-faced policeMAN
bubble-lipped and bubble-eyed
nudges Johnson with his twirly baton night stick
—MOVE ON, NIGGA—"
We all heard that shit before.

"time stops for the classic scene
the players, righteous brothas and sistas
immobilized by anger
and resignation, wait

"a pink freckled white "lady" there shopping for sights
speaks on Johnson's behalf
as if the street map she fanned with a gloved hand was
a letter of introduction
her eyes ventured from the policeMAN's smirk
to Johnson's stone face
she stood on the corner enraptured
after the policeMAN resumed vigilant stroll
the sound of Johnson's mellifluous voice
unbuttoned her summer-thin floral print dress
unhooked, unfastened her
she stepped out of the pool of silk, lace, and cotton

"Johnson tried not to see her inside his poem
thought about his women
sistas brown sugar-brown
lips reminiscent of cinnamon, honey

I don't think y'all heard me. Hmph. I said
"Johnson tried not to see her inside his poem
thought about HIS women
sistas brown sugar-brown
cinnamon, honey sistas

"she tilted toward him
he thought HARD and SPIT—

"she felt the warm glob, smack her abdomen
trail down into her wispy pubes

"he took out his dick, lengthening with rage

"she gyrated rhythmless desire
anticipating a black man's thrusting kiss

"so he pissed
up into her face
imagining her pouty bird
lips around him
her legs thrown up to Jesus
his shudder nutting into her ass

"whoever brought her there grabbed her
clothes and took her away
Ezekiel, the corner grocer, muttered the collective sentiment
—crazy white bitch—"

(awkward pause)

This piece of poem is a backpocket love song, twenty times folded, edges worn gray. Damn, curvaceous Nile sistas of luscious limbs and openings, Johnson is a poet, author of earth's first breath, imparting knowledge because our history is not biodegradable! THIS is some SEMINAL shit!

(the dashiki men stomp, whistle
(the poet leaves the stage with echoes of musty male voices in his head
(like when he was twelve, after school in the alley
(going for the panties
(hi-fives to his boys, nodding to the sistas
(he feels for the elastic ridge, the damp crotch

(and the women with angry hair sit clapping
(ignoring their own bodies
(locked kink fight of their natural hair
(forgetting slaves' picking fingers
(ancestors sexless in the field, on the tree
(forgetting history
(forgetting

Water from the Well

for Duriel Fannie Pilgrim Gault

I have your name: wholly holy, Hebrew
resonance softened by slur of introduction:
of the light of God. Angel warrior. Celebration.

They called you Dura. Mama Beulah named you after a cousin:
D U R I E L, Durle. Letters lazy in field heat. Holler through hills.
What southern tongues twisted with slow indifference, my mother coaxed
upright to give to me: Duriel. Anointing. Chubby brown girlchild
born into memory's bold revision. Now I am a woman
whose dreams extend backward into shadows: I feel
my way through language to arrive at a deserted border town.

You are my grandmother. You are on the other side: that's how I came
to have your name. This is all I know.

Someone tells me that you will come to me in my sleep if I call to you.

So I sprinkle rosewater on my pillow and go to bed, wanting
to hear the timbre of your voice, wanting to smell the line-dry linen
of your dresses. I go to bed listening for porch boards' creak, trying to imagine
the smell of peach tree blossoms and the earth flavor of red clay dirt.

One night you step from the other side
into my room, a stretch of ripe cotton rows.
I see you across the way. Your apron, dusted with flour.
We are up on the mountain, in granddaddy's fields. I am skipping
barelegged in a yellow dress balancing an empty tin wash tub on my hip.
Now we're nearer the house. I'm squeeze-yanking cow udders
but there's nothing to catch the milk so it spills into dirt.
I'm in the front room; you are water-waving your hair.
Now it's winter and my chest is tight as cold molasses. I'm in bed
under a handmade quilt, shivering. Goose grease popping on the stove.
You are wringing supper's chicken necks, hands soft white
from wash water. You are singing pillowcases from flour sacks.
You are teaching the stitch with your eyes
closed. Colored Cherokee woman. I am sweeping ashes
near the wood stove, humming quartet songs and "Mississippi
Po' Boy." I am sent giggling to the well for water.

When I return I am carrying nothing
but your name

and you are gone.

4th movement

Villanelle
for the dead white fathers

Backwater, yeah, but I ain't wet, so misters, I ain't studin' you:
Don't need your blessed doctrine to tell me what to write and when.
Behold, God made me funky. There ain't nothin' I cain't do.

I can write frontpocket Beale Street make you sweat and crave the blues,
Dice a hymnal 'til you shout *Glory! The Holy Ghost done sent me sin!*
Backwater, yeah, but I ain't wet, so misters, I ain't studin' you:

Signify a sonnet—to the boil of "Bitches Brew."
Rhyme royal a triolet, weave sestina's thick through thin.
I said God made me funky. There ain't nothin' I cain't do.

Eeshabbabba a subway station from damnation to upper room.
Lift-swing-hunh chain gang hammer like Alabama's nigga men.
Backwater, yeah, but I ain't wet, so misters, I ain't studin' you:

Shish kebab heroic couplets and serve 'em dipped in barbecue,
Slap-bass blank-verse-lines, tunin' fork tines 'til you think I'm Milton's kin.
Indeed, God made me funky. There ain't nothin' I cain't do.

You're poets dead; I'm poet live. Darky choruses belt: *Hallelu'.*
While you were steppin' out, someone else was steppin' in.
Backwater, yeah, but I ain't wet, so misters, I ain't studin' you:
God sho-nuff sho-nuff made me funky. There ain't nan thing I cain't do.

Wise Fool Evolution or 1/2 the battle
a Double Bop
for Jabari Khalid Muhammad, Dan Sullivan, & Dennis Sangmin Kim

Inedible revolution: wise fools hoof-and-mouth to "free-range rude"
solutions / (Self-despise and antagonize the best of us, impede the rest
of us) / Blind to the connections, never to see their reflections on
"Lifestyles" / (except to grace the inside of a condom) / Their wisdom as
faulty as their scared sweat stench is salty / Magazine imaginings of pine
box groupies / Chock-fulla-lead, dred, can't wait to be jail and casket bait /
Catchin hell in a handbasket

Heard the word, D / *We can and will become what we aspire to be*[1]

We wanna be spendin it without winnin it / Winded and spinnin shit webs
without toilets / Kismet freestyle zeros, no shows in mirrors—so so deaf /
G-Fool brags a 3x5 glossary, one word philosophy / Monosyllabic: strained
and pureed for the fool palate / Ignoring synonyms that could be
befriendin him / Such as victuals and cranium, instead G meditates on
platinum / Fantasizing luxury via usury and buggery

Hear the word, G
We can and will become what we aspire to be

*There'll come a time when the world won't be singing / Flowers won't grow
and the bells won't be ringing / Who really cares, who is willing to try? / Who'll
save a world that is destined to die? / Save the babies ...*[2] / *Hmph* / *Give it up,
turn it loose / It's not worth it ...*[3] / But there'll come a time

Hear the word, B
Re-search your biography, auto-graph your phylogeny
We can and will become what we aspire to be

So, free your mind and your ass will follow / Cash is hollow and the
converse is also true / Shoot up your TV, make it o.d./ Media cracks, kills
your culture / Sucks your soul into a hole—so so deep / One arrow and no
tomorrow / Bad boys, bad boys bring da noise and your ducats but / you
can't cop it without pockets and the reaper is clockin you

Re-search your biography

Free your ass and your mind will follow / Beware the wallow and mire of funkless fronting / Remember one thing: hallowed be the knowledge in the kingdom of the soul / Discern the goal: love is the message and the groove lessons, so listen / (okay that's two things) and before you do things / Flip the script on the verbiage—be silent / (be silent)

Re-search your biography, auto-graph your phylogeny / (be sage, be righteous)
Re-search your biography, auto-graph your phylogeny / (be peace)
We can and will become what we aspire to be

---

[1] from "Heaven's Here on Earth" as performed by Tracy Chapman
[2] from "Someday We'll All Be Free/Save the Children" as performed by Regina Belle
[3] from "Give It Up, Turn It Loose" as performed by En Vogue

Awakening

Wind is in the cane. Come along.
Cane leaves swaying, rusty with talk,
Scratching choruses above the guinea's squawk,
Wind is in the cane. Come along.
                    —Jean Toomer, from "Carma"

I. Proem

We begin   with
the sucking of teeth
a name compressed, squeezed
of its vowels, a number,
a disembodied imperative
answered by letters to God,
loose laughter of scattered half-notes,
staccato of ripened-too-soon

We   memory
begin with proclamation, fighting
the suck of smallness in all
things manifest, scratching drought
at the openings, encroaching

We be/gin with debt
and necessity, power,
praisesong, orisha
riding air and magic
likened to madness, light,
a daughter's geography

I was born in a cane field
I was born in a cotton field
in a brake
in the thick of thieves
on the way
back from the sudden dead

We memory
begin self/   estranged
fruitless, pruned into missing
orphaned of the ground,
deserving, We be/gin

re/membering
harvest cries, inventing
and celebrating this
perpetual present, *me*
for my recitative self
me for my recitative

II. Creation

Strange woman, I fall asleep
after the world has been created
into the crease between female and Eve,
ribwoman, gift. This day, awakening,
beside my brown body, traversing
the surface, I linger, caressing
rough places and scars, familiar blemishes
and new moles, spider-veined thighs,
bumps of coiled hair, plumb-stone breasts.
I watch my body breathe, being. I see
the part others see: the periphery. The rind.
This day, awakening, as a ghost spit up from the river,
precious to myself if to none other, I am the story
of the blank-bellied woman, the story of her name,
and its brass box secret calling to me
where I wait to be born. I am in accordance
with my purpose. Spun out to the perimeter.
Radiating breath's momentum
I return singing.

Drive

Cool night, like the snap of peas or dry branches underfoot.
Someone's waiting for me: a photograph of my breath.
The moon is cropped stingy and my skin is a tethered shade of heat
drawn to outer darkness and the gentle sucking in the thick of it.

Looking for the turn. Dull stretch of road the weight
of any other. Rolling straight back into clannish trees
like a cinnamon woman, powdered cleavage, struck
dumb in the spirit, falls back trusting.

A dredloc creeps from behind my ear, scrapes my nose, yarn
between my eyes. I slip its tight coil into place with a motion
reminiscent of white girls' easy laughter and the prep school I hated,
tinged with the riddle of their dearness and my brown body unseen.

Looking for the turn. Sign posts become tar field scarecrows,
mute Colored, bowed heads at 3 a.m. wherever trees shoot up
in a clearing. And down a piece there's a church, one room sanctuary,
one paint-chipped iron rail at the front three steps. The doors

are swollen shut from rain; above them, a cross-shaped window
broken out, fist-sized, where Jesus' head would be.
Cool night passes through the jagged godhead whistling,
condenses on the stained glass pane the way a house settles,

the way our bodies soften into earth, the way our suffering
mists, seeps into the bloodstream and runs. My we,
us, we people breathing on both sides of the hold belly.
Greed and our flesh trials nursed the second half of the last millennium.

What I wouldn't do for a bidi. I turn on the radio.
There. And I'll turn again before I reach the leaf dense trees
to go where I'll spend the night. Haven, where someone's waiting
and smells like cornbread under cloth, like thighs, moist

armpits, is a double portion, ribbed, combed, and fastened.
At the end of it: a bell my fingers feel for.
Sometimes, I dream a lonely highway and wake up driving;
sometimes, I am wet and full and prone in the pasture.

While inside me, desire shepherds the hills swallowing night's crisp
center and loose pearls in the swayback of darkness until I
breathe, reaching, replenished, forgetting, palpable
and palatable like pulling smoke but more than momentary

shuttling lungs and ear drums, more than, until I am a dream
within a dream within a dream like electric organ humpbacks
and only-born-once Al Green's happiness squealing
eeeeeeeeee moan for love eeeeeeeee over road hiss

over dirt shoulder scratches over prairie far off trees and sky
darknesses taking up space until I am an ellipsis, spinning.

Jive from the Velvet
Sugar Kinky Quatrains Plus 1
for Harryette Mullen & Douglas Ewart

<u>Refrain/Punch/Hook</u>
ssssshhhugar tit inventions sho nuff
cane break molasses
haints' loc drum lashes
my high brow blow

<u>1st shot</u>
engine drag on discordant snatch
an eye fool icon yr mind zone ice
twice gone crazy pimp shady ghetto bait
hook-a-ho-n-go gimme one tow
        (to those)

        ssssshhhugar tit inventions sho nuff
        cane break molasses
        haints' loc drum lashes
        my high brow blow

<u>try it again, brim</u>
dungeon whatcha done done son
shine on my game—show me the snake
sign shake-throat jimmy open omen last
nightlight dim cracker D-deck stacked
        (wit)

        ssssshhhugar tit show
                nuf blow

<u>slo mo' time, cat daddy</u>

dat	mini	disk	slip	skidittitty	shit	
strangy	thang	gee	he	be	ridin	me
citysilly	jack	an	dis	housewear	else	I
sheet	blankets	bull	—let's	scheme-sing		

        ssssshhhugar tit fits

60

neo-soul trick-drop bling bling hook
lil man quatrain bus fare wish bone eye
balla money holla at the honies' two-door corners
rockin copper wheelie free meal feelie
happy patch sniff-n-scratch—really?
        (ha! don't trip!)

so: umph. there you go video ho-ing, boing boing
what you smoke broke down and used parts
you can't play your instrument that way uptown
this way gig, dig ditty spade, spare shade can't fade
my pomo promo [video ho] shhhhhit

Crazy Woman Blues

I ain't never left Chicago
But I been around the world
Spent every day in dis here city
But I'se traveled 'round the world
Got me a crazy woman
And she done took me fo' a twirl
(Usedta picture myself lucky
To court a Southside Chi-town girl)

Got me a crazy woman
Put me out but won't let me go
Got me a pretty crazy woman
Throw me out the front
      Then drag me through the back door
She make up her first mind—quick
But she got a dozen mo' to go
(Say she got mo' n one mind
But don't you tell her I said so)

Quick—not easy—she fix her first mind
To love me right and love me true
Claim she made it in her right mind
To love me mo'n my mama do
When I reckon all I done for her
Make me think I'm crazy, too
(I need to shake this rattlin' woman
All the shit she put me through)

When I reckon what I ain't yet done
I thinks to do it by myself
When I adds up what I ain't yet seen
Need mo' fingers than I got left
Fifty ways to leave a lover
Need a dead ringer to put her down
(Don't you dare go off an' warn her
Or I'll put you in the ground
(Ya know I'se jivin' 'bout that last part
Ya know the way I likes to clown))

But straight an' skinny, don't go laughin'
Don't shoot yo' mouth off all through town
She got mo' ears than she got minds
And she keeps 'em to the ground
That woman's eyes is like a hawk's
So don't go foolin' her aroun'
(Pray to God you never meet her
Or you'll *wish* you was in the ground)

Pray to yo' God you never meet her
If you do—you don't know me
Pray on three knees you never meet her
If you do—you ain't *seen* me
I'm off to merry England,
For dried up biscuits, beef and tea
Change my name to Jean-Pierre
And wander 'round in gay Pa-ri
(Find me another crazy woman
In polite society)

"
...
b
l
u
e
s

c
o
m
e

f
r
o
m

a

w
o
m
a
n

w
a
n
t

i
n
g

t
o

s
e
e

h
e
r

m
a
n

a
n
d

a

m
a
n

w
a
n
t

i
n
g

t
o

s
e
e

h
i
s

w
o
m
a
n
"

F
u
r
r
y

L
e
w
i
s

Trois

Blues Sestina Rhapsody

(down home grit, gut-n-jelly
roll, switch-n-stagger woman
scratch your name into my soul
stitch-n-swagger woman
love your mendin til I'm old

found her a dagger woman
stab me soon as I came home
black snake limp from riding country
hard leg whittled to the bone

good woman turned
good woman gone
good woman turned
good woman gone

turned

gone

64

Recess

i.
leave what cannot be carried

ii.
this coupling: steam, cool water
trickle of sighs

press	nipple	palm	arc
ask	warm	wrists	grasp
press	pubes	pulse	need
nestle	breathe	breasts	yes
breaking	trace	waking	yes

waking to her: my belly taut,
lift and shiver. *there, too!*
sing the body chords
lengthening to fill
space between seizure and air

iii.
who raises the latch?
who waits at the sill?

iv.
meadow
woodland cottage
stained glass sky

the gate is open
        doors behind mirrors
        mirrors behind doors

roughhousing
no *holes* barred
no seed unspent

small men
smaller boy
        scuffed   frayed   vanishing

manhood pouched sticky in his fist
cloud-milk mixed in blood

    difficult words:
    splayed rectum

        quiver

            kiss

v.
who sees what bubbles from the ground?
who fastens the shutter?

a simple choreography

necessity
        beckons
                comes

5th movement

Voice of America

Peckerwood Creek, Alabama (no blacks no jews no gays):
Billy Jack Gater is dead forever   *sissy*
("Blinded by Hatred" 20/20) The way he sees it, killer owns the story
cause he ain't dead
Nina's singin in me   and ain't no sugar   ain't gonna be no sugar

Mississippi   Mississippi   Mississippi
Mississippi   Got Damn   Mississippi
Nina's singin in me   and ain't no sugar   ain't gonna be none

Remember that
fictive shadow: gritty   muddy   blue lit: forest hutting
make it dark-dark darker than that and barbed
call that story song, hear that ravenous absence
no secret hunger   built to last
Nina's singin   and ain't no sugar

Black Gator   felled by jungle fever
was no martyr   was a misstep
in da dance   da dee da daaa
doin it to death
pi_e in the pocket, in the pocket
blood in the pocket book play(s) dozens
cha ching!: dollar signs and since
Nina's singin in me   ain't no sugar   ain't gonna be no sugar

Ask Mississippi
this set's in the street   milk crate in the road
sampled discord dat swingin pulp
obscenity in your living   room in the measure
rest to mark   *beat*   time is an accessory
we cannot afford

Persistent ideology makes itself
known   *we are American*   and valued
and the church said   ; universal truths rest
in the value   *use and leisure*   placed
on certain inalienable bodies:
Better to reign in Hell, that story

Whatcha want   whatcha want   two dimes and a nickel
Whatcha want want you, Walk on
Whatcha want   whatcha want   half a mind to get it
Whatcha want want you, Walk on

If there is one true word uttered here:
nigger—its monstrous possibilities—variations
and axioms: axes: n I g (g) (a) (h) (z)
no sugar

      [5 year old South Africa wards 3 oceans, trades 6 billion bones for submarines.
      Her men are taking their women by force.   theirs [italics]
      And who would have thought 3 letters could keep
      still as sleep   (each little death)   so much blood in them.
      3 letters   *praxis* : a free state's pass to pandemic affection.
      The orphan sea will avenge its mother's body.

      Where is Nelson Mandela
      Tear down the shantytown: he's home
      Bring back Nelson Mandela
      Tear down the shantytown: he's home]   no sugar

no fallen back into old music, everything a woman
scorned, loose, chaste, plain, shapely
a looker, with a car, a hooker, a nun
tight-tight, ready to pop, born to be ____ed
sanctified, mammy, sapphire, hot
bitchy, tired, tested, tried, true
a digger, a dame, a queen, a skeeze
luck, a chicken, cold, a tease
muse hoochie, muse goddess, moody muse
mule
let go   *ya oughta let it go*
woman singin   ain't no sugar

Ask somebody
who owns it ain't dead
foot on the neck, that story
Sugar Ditch, Mississippi
rumored kin Westside Hypewalk #____
Chicago, Illinois   *Mississippi*

70

25 below too cold to ho
25 below too cold to ho
Never too cold to pimp

Money won't change you
In time, Sugar   *In time*

Nothing is real to us but hunger
—Kakuzo Okakura

fragments of a last song
for Al Preciado, sculptor

i.
O mundo coberto de penas.

ii.
Thorny howling dog, the kiln is hot.

                    Orfeo, come with me
to the house of my husband. Beloved, risen
from the urn, come with me to the gypsy.
I will ride, majestic, in the silt of your open mouth.

Howling dog, peg teeth, standing bull-thick,
ready for the kiln. I call you Baleia
to resurrect faith spirits fleshed swollen
swept by the undertow of *vidas secas.*

       Baleia had yelped desperately at our heels.
       Her clawed dirt circles, reminiscences of a meal.
       Her small lean body, skinned and stiff,
         its cavern split by crackle and spit.

           Dusk. Fire husked, hollow:
           :tough meat wanting savor.

Vía y vida, secas.

iii.
I gave my first daughter to my mother on the third day.

For nine days, I dream of skeletons in white coats.
Their jaws are wired shut and moths light in their eye sockets.
In a white-tiled corner, a hand of air draws light from my mouth.
The light rises in loaves.

Reckoning

In some other world, the sea envelops the sand
and the sand, the sea. Imagined island poem

where serenity blooms so vividly we cannot
name it. Reef coral, beaded scar, beckoning

beginnings that rise soft, oval, still forming.
Nearer, road-callused, our feet become our house.

Doorless brickening. One window
to leap from. Peace, the name that window knows.

Undersong. Blue grass. Hip-high surf.
Dream wave faces breaking into laughter.

Untethered, unhinged, we walk their tongues to the tips
as day vanishes into salt and gull notes.

Peace, falling into possibility beneath sleep
where we speak gradients of sky and sea

and press bolts of memory in ink.

she is like a road—pretty, but crooked
                —Kenyan proverb

40 women
for Julia Query
because although we love our mothers, we cannot live for them

move
Aní-Yun´wiya   we are calumet
mudança   mudança-ungh
jabarigáni:nia   jabarigáni:nia

dada   dadeedlelee dada
de mí tierra bella   Afríka
me nah shut me mout   me nah tap shout
tahk tickey tickey tahk   doom´dah

move
Aní-Yun´wiya   we are weeping eye
mudança   mudança-ungh
jabarigáni:nia   jabarigáni:nia

dadeedlelee dada   daaaaaaaa
de mí tierra santa   Afríka
me nah shut me mout   me nah tap shout
tahk tickey tickey tahk   doom´dah

Rodrigo's little **black** book o'rhymes
tr. anon

Americana (34)

hanky panky
ugly and stanky
chimps denied poontang are cranky

move   move
Aní-Yun´wiya   we are calumet   Aní-Yun´wiya   we are weeping eye
mudança   mudança-ungh   mudança   mudança-ungh
jabarigáni:nia   jabarigáni:nia   jabarigáni:nia   jabarigáni:nia

little black dress (*SkyMall*)

Custom Molded Ankle & Heel Support
(Grout Whitener)
Custom Home Bleaching Kit
~~Waistband Stretcher~~
AB Dolly 2
Cincher
24 Pocket Pantry Organizer
Bike Lift System
Moisturizing Gloves, Socks
Bikini Trimmer
(Non-Skid Auto Exec, Retracting Modem Card)
Full Bench Pet Seat (Protector)—Black
Nasal Clip Snoring Aid
Laundry Sorter
Hamper Deodorizer
Magnetic Shoulder Wrap
Bucky™ (Travel Pillow)

move   move
de mí tierra bella   Afrika   de mí tierra santa   Afrika
Ani-Yun'wiya   we are calumet   Ani-Yun'wiya   we are weeping eye
me nah shut me mout me nah tap shout   me nah shut me mout me nah tap shout

TRADING CARD(S)

Sunburned Am.™

Lor bress yo' honey!
Whar yo' gwine?
Yo' s'uttnly am
lookin fine!

Dem closes you got
mus be de bait
to make some niggah
keep a date!

move		move	
Aní-Yun´wiya	we are calumet	Aní-Yun´wiya	we are weeping eye
mudança	mudança-ungh	mudança	mudança-ungh
jabarigáni:nia	jabarigáni:nia	jabarigáni:nia	jabarigáni:nia

living bodies

omega
[...]
alpha

```
move                                          move
Aní-Yun´wiya         we are calumet           Aní-Yun´wiya         we are weeping eye
mudança              mudança-ungh             mudança              mudança-ungh
jabarigáni:nia       jabarigáni:nia           jabarigáni:nia       jabarigáni:nia


dada                 dadeedlelee dada         dadeedlelee dada     daaaaaaaa
de mí tierra bella   Afríka                   de mí tierra santa   Afríka
me nah shut me mout  me nah tap shout         me nah shut me mout  me nah tap shout
tahk tickey tickey tahk  doom´dah             tahk tickey tickey tahk  doom´dah
```

I will answer you, and will tell you great and hidden things that you have not known

—Jeremiah

Phou

i.
I want to blow my brains out. How many times have I said this:
Out, taut smog. Out, shadow. Coarse white cloth, billowing.

> *phou, the pilot breathes in sleep.*

                    clean.

what is real is my capacity to damage and to heal.
what is real is my choice between two
and the way I oscillate, measuring.

ii.
once I sent a woman into the street to wait.

4 AM Brooklyn heat. She called the cab and went down; I canceled it.
From the window, I watched her waiting and pacing, smoking a cigarette
nervously, then another. Brooklyn trees are known to block street lamps
and passageways. Outside you could not see what moved until it was upon
you.

Now and again a hoopty livery cab would chuckle along, rolling its heavy
engine: *Goodie-bye,* it would say like mythical Ibo flying away, leaving her
put cause she didn't have no wings, just feet, and they were swollen from
salt and cracked and pudgy the way feet can be like sausage, the ends of
things stuffed into skin. I watched her from upstairs and went down,
kindly asked if she'd like me to call again because I would, because even
though I was sending her away something in me wished to be kind. Still
she waited, out in the street flicking a cigarette staring into the maw of
Murder Ave. She dug around the tree bricks with her piggish feet, clawing
at shit. For how many minutes can a woman wait for a cab in the 4am
dark away from the city's yellow zooming? *Phou.* She walked to the
corner and on. I didn't feel bad. We both knew she was stupid to hoof it
toward Fulton Street that late: anyone could snatch her out of the air and
bludgeon her head into suffocation, balled point, stain. Did I suspect she

would hail a drunken cabby and ride hellbound home? Did I care? She
deserved. She had earned it and the world could give it to her. Yes, we
could give it to her.

iii.

> *Satisfaction is being where you belong, just warm enough,*
> *just full enough to forget where your skin ends and the world begins.*

iv.
On the screen, the 4-year-old boy squirms
beneath the man. His red cap, his bicycle:
caught. Little red riding hood: the man
opens his fly just enough to get it out,
get it in.

> *O veil of the sanctuary.*

The man's ecstatic peeling rips, from rafter to board.
This time, red is eaten by the woodsman. There is no wolf, just me.

phou.

Other Titles From Elixir Press

Nomadic Foundations
  Sandra Meek
  0-9709342-3-8 • $13

Flow Blue
  Sarah Kennedy
  0-9709342-5-4 • $13

Monster Zero
  Jay Snodgrass
  0-9709342-6-2 • $13

Circassian Girl
  Michelle Mitchell-Foust
  0-9709342-2-X • $13

Distance From Birth
  Tracy Philpot
  0-9709342-1-1 • $13